Acknowledgement

This Advent season, I meditate on the meaning of heavenly hope. Should I explain why? Nope. I do not even need to mention how difficult our pandemic challenges have been. We have lost some of our beloved families and friends. And every day we listen to heart-breaking news. Then, the hardest part of this troubled moment is to see conflict and emotional challenges within our society. And . . . it is still going on.

But, the environment when the baby Jesus was born was not different. Today's reader may understand this birth story of Christmas as one of adorable historic events, and it must be the most joyful moment of our human history. However, the truth was different. Socio-economic archeological research has explained that Jews were living under Roman Empire and their life was not easy. Even though Jewish people understood themselves as God's selected people, *chosen ones*, they had to accept their painful reality. The Roman Empire ruled over their territory and charged every Jew to pay lots of tax. Even their own Jewish local officials took advantage even more by giving them double burdens. More and more ordinary people became tenant farmers because they could not afford their taxes and financial difficulties anymore.

Then read this advent story in the Bible again. A young girl was pregnant, and her brave fiancé did not hesitate to join this challenging journey with her. Moreover, they had to travel to their hometown to register their names while they expected their baby soon. The weather got colder and they knew they did not have enough money to lodge. Did they expect to book a cozy inn to stay? I doubt it.

Today, we may see the same challenges and hardships of the Advent story. But we know the coming of Baby Jesus is the undeniable evidence of heavenly hope for all. It becomes a powerful message because people could find hope in the midst of real challenges in their lives. They continuously called the name of the Lord, and prayed that they would see the salvation of God. Then Jesus came to this world and now we are excited to see the same hope that people found two thousand years ago. Find the baby Jesus in your life, then you will see God's hope is still with us.

Ward's Chapel is a loving congregation, and they always enjoy sharing their faithful testimonies. This is one of the powerful ministries that they do even during the pandemic age. Then this year, the church published its first Lenten devotional and they decided to continue to make their first Advent devotional as well. As a pastor of this congregation, I am always delighted to read their life testimonies and faithful stories. That's because the stories that I read and heard are real; real voices from our beloved witnesses. This Advent season, I hope this daily devotion will help you encounter spiritual moments of your life so that you can find a meaningful call and message from God.

Sing a joyful song, God's son is with us!

Ward's Chapel UMC (Randallstown MD)
Rev. Dr. Steven Cho

Monday, November 29, 2021

Steven Cho
(Pastor)

Luke 3:7-11
New Revised Standard Version
[7] John said to the crowds that came out to be baptized by him, "You brood of vipers! Who warned you to flee from the wrath to come? [8] Bear fruits worthy of repentance. Do not begin to say to yourselves, 'We have Abraham as our ancestor'; for I tell you, God is able from these stones to raise up children to Abraham. [9] Even now the ax is lying at the root of the trees; every tree therefore that does not bear good fruit is cut down and thrown into the fire." [10] And the crowds asked him, "What then should we do?" [11] In reply he said to them, "Whoever has two coats must share with anyone who has none; and whoever has food must do likewise."

Reflection:
In our passage today, we see John the Baptist rebuked the crowds, and it sounds so harsh, "You brood of vipers." Have you ever heard these comments in your congregations or during your worship? Then you would not listen to these types of words. I know it is hard to take.
Then, John kept telling them the reason. "Bear fruits worthy of repentance. Do not begin to say to yourselves, 'We have Abraham as our ancestor'; for I tell you, God is able from these stones to raise up children to Abraham." The crowds that John the Baptist was talking to were so proud of the fact that they were descendants of

Abraham, and they knew they were chosen people; God blessed Israel!

However, John pointed out that they missed something important. He directly asked them if they had lived as faithful believers, if they did good things, if they reached out to people in need, if they shared the love of God. He did not ask about the background in which they were raised, nor the religious environment in which they grew up, but about the faithful fruit that they produced. Yes, bearing fruit is a key. Bearing good fruit! Do the right things for the kingdom of God.

I still listen to the questions of the crowds in our passage. They repeatedly said, "What should we do?". I believe it is a good start to make a meaningful change during this Advent season. As we recall the reason why God sent His son, and the example that Jesus showed us, we may ask ourselves the same question of the people during this Advent season: "What should we do as the children of God?"

Prayer:
Gracious and loving God. We thank you for the time and moment that we kneel down before you and meditate on your message today. Give us your wisdom and help us have deeper knowledge to know the reason why you sent your son. We pray in your name amen.

Tuesday, November 30, 2021

1 Peter 5: 6-7
Humble yourselves, then, under God's mighty hand, so that He will lift you up in his own good time. Leave all your worries with him, because he cares for you.

Reflection:

In this Christmas season, as well as in past years, one word that always becomes foremost in my mind is "humble." When you consider the circumstances of Jesus's birth, how can anyone look upon this event and not be impressed by its simplicity, its modesty, and yes, its utter humility? Where else have you ever heard of a king being born in a lowly stable? It begs the question of why God chose the birth of his son to take place in such surroundings.

It becomes clear as you read the Bible that Jesus's humble birth is consistent with the high value that God places on the quality of humility. Indeed, the entire lifetime of Jesus here on earth, not just his birth, was marked by its simple, humble lifestyle. We know from numerous Bible verses, both old and new testament, that God resists the proud and provides grace for the humble. Humility is the ability to be without pride or arrogance and is a principal characteristic of those who follow Jesus Christ. Jesus is the best example of someone who humbly followed God's plan for him. But apart from this example are many mentions in the Bible of the importance of humility before God.

For example:
Old Testament:

Psalm 149.4: "For the Lord takes delight in his people; he crowns the humble with victory."
Proverbs 3:34: "He mocks proud mockers, but shows favor to the humble and oppressed."

New Testament:
Matthew 23: 11-12: "The greatest among you will be your servant. For those who exalt themselves will be humbled, and those who humble themselves will be exalted."
James 4:6: "But he gives us more grace. That is why Scripture says: 'God opposes the proud but shows favor to the humble."

So as we celebrate in the season upon us, let us be mindful that the humble circumstances of Jesus's birth are part of God's plan, and a lesson for all of us in how our Lord expects us to conduct ourselves here on Earth. Remember that any and all blessings we receive during this joyous season are from God's grace, and we should humbly acknowledge this in our thoughts and prayers.

Prayer:
Lord, during this Christmas season, help us to recall the lesson in humility we learn from Jesus' birth. Please grant us the same meekness and humility, because it is through these qualities that we are able to serve the sick, the oppressed, and the least of our brothers and sisters here on earth. Remove from us the desire to be praised by others. May we desire others to be esteemed more than us. We pray for this through Jesus Christ, our Lord and Savior. Amen.

Wednesday, December 1, 2021

Barb Charnock
(Lay Leader)

Lamentations 5:19
19 You, LORD, reign forever; your throne endures from generation to generation.

Reflection:
Jeremiah understood that God knew all the terrible things that had happened to Jerusalem, but he feared God had forgotten them. Even worse, he feared God was unfair in punishing them and not the fathers who had brought these calamities upon them. In the end of his lamentations, Jeremiah returns to his faith that God is "eternal and unchanging with his throne enduring from generation to generation." As Hebrews 13:8 would say later "Jesus is the same yesterday, today and forever."

Jeremiah petitions God to turn him and his people back to God "unless you have utterly rejected us and are very angry with us." The key thought here is that it is God who gives us the gift of repentance, not ourselves. God is the *turner* who will complete their repentance and restore them personally and as a nation.

We know God is the same yesterday, today and forever. We have those words emblazoned on the wall of our Fellowship Hall. Then, from where does the constant worry, doubt and questioning come in our lives each day? We are both cursed and gifted with a human nature that compels these thoughts. We mistakenly assume that all this *lamenting* will buy us peace. It does not. Only our faith in God's great love for us and his desire to *turn* us to him gives us peace and releases us from the anxiety that

Jeremiah epitomized. Fortunately, neither Israel's nor our story ends with lamentations. We are Jesus' people so we know just how much God loved us and how much God sacrificed to turn us back to him.

Prayer:

Our Heavenly Father, we gratefully turn to you and accept your gift of repentance. When we see your Son on the cross, we are reminded of just how much you love us. Help us to be worthy of that eternal love and acceptance and extend it to our neighbors. We love because you first loved us and we see reminders of that love every day. Thank you, Father, for that sustaining love. Amen.

Thursday, December 2, 2021

Ben Palmer

1 Samuel 12:24
24 But be sure to fear the LORD and serve him faithfully with all your heart; consider what great things he has done for you.

Reflection:
While growing up, I heard the terminology regarding *fearing* God both in general conversation and during sermons while attending church. My understanding was that it seemed to be a favorable comment for someone to refer to another as a "God-fearing person." As a child I almost always accepted the literal meaning of a word and left little to interpretation. So, I wondered why anyone would fear God. Why should we fear God who provides for us and extends his blessings on all of us for our success and prosperity?

Later in life I realized that having a *fear* of God most likely referred to the deep, profound respect and love that we all should have for our Creator. For some this realization happens very easily, and yet for others, this realization takes more time and, perhaps, more life experiences. However, God's great plan for each and every one of us is to grow in the Spirit at a pace which he desires us to grow. Growing to fear God and realizing the blessings God provides for us every day requires a degree of open-mindedness and willingness to believe what may or may not be easily seen.

In a world where it seems that good constantly struggles to overcome evil, we are so fortunate to have a strong community of faith where we can share our own personal successes and struggles. I believe that sharing our experiences and beliefs emboldens others to follow the will of God and is part of his plan to allow us to grow our fear of him. My hope is that we all continue down the path of realizing the blessings God has bestowed upon us and that we will have the ability to influence others so that they realize God's blessings upon them.

Prayer:

Heavenly Father, thank you for all the blessings that you have afforded us, both seen and unseen. We ask that you continue to bless us so that we can faithfully and dutifully spread your message as you have guided us. Give us the ability to realize and understand to the greatest extent allowable your blessings as witness to your creation. Provide opportunities for us to continue to grow our fear of you and assist others in that growth. We ask all these in the name of your Son, Jesus. Amen.

Friday, December 3, 2021

Hosea 6:3

3 Let us acknowledge the LORD; let us press on to acknowledge him. As surely as the sun rises, he will appear; he will come to us like the winter rains, like the spring rains that water the earth."

Reflection:

As I read this verse, it rang so true to my life and how I try to live. I acknowledge the Lord every day through prayer, through my actions and through the ways I try to live my life. I give thanks to the Lord for all my blessings, of which there are many. Each day when I pray I acknowledge that I could not make it through trying times without his help. He does appear in my life to give me strength when I need it and to take away my fears. When I need guidance and someone to show me the way when I am troubled, he comes to me and guides and directs me. I always know that he will appear in my life and provide the many blessings like the winter and spring rains that water the earth; he nourishes my soul and renews my faith.

Prayer:

Dear Lord, thank you for the many blessings you provide to each of us. We acknowledge you and thank you. May we always remain faithful and live life to serve you, Lord. We know you will appear in our lives as surely as the sun rises. May we recognize your many gifts and acknowledge you as our Lord every day of our lives. Amen.

Saturday, December 4, 2021

Bridget Wetzel
(Preschool Director)

2 Peter 3:10
¹⁰ But the day of the Lord will come like a thief. The heavens will disappear with a roar; the elements will be destroyed by fire, and the earth and everything done in it will be laid bare."

Reflection:

In the Advent season of preparation, we must remember, too, that we should also be making ready for Jesus Christ to come again. Peter defends God's promise of the Lord's return. Judgement *will* come, but we don't know when. It will come like a thief in the night, without warning, so be prepared and live as if we know this to be true.

God reminds us that the end will come, even as we celebrate the beginning in this Christmas season. He wants us to be prepared. He wants all his children to be saved.

I try to live by Jesus' example every day, though some days are harder than others. Nobody is perfect, but I know in my heart that I am a good person and strive to do good each day. I think I'm prepared and I think that God would approve of how I've lived my life. When the day of the Lord comes, will you be ready?

Prayer:

Lord, thank you for letting us know that there will be an end even as we celebrate a beginning. Peter reminds us that we should live each day as a reflection of Jesus' example. I believe that a day of reckoning will be coming. Make me worthy and ready for that unknown day that Jesus will return so that I am not surprised by its arrival. Amen.

Sunday, December 5, 2021

Psalm 118:24
The LORD has done it this very day; let us rejoice today and be glad.

Enjoy your Sunday worship!

Sunday Humor

Jesus and Moses are golfing.
Jesus says, "Watch this drive. It'll be just like Tiger Woods."
He hits the ball and it lands in the lake.
Moses says, "I'll get it." He goes down to the lake, parts the water and retrieves the ball.
"Okay," Jesus says, "This time, it WILL be just like Tiger Woods." He hits the ball and again, it lands in the lake.
Moses goes down, parts the lake and retrieves the ball.
"Third time is a charm," Jesus says. "Watch, just like Tiger Woods." And for the third time he hits the ball into the lake.
Moses says, "This time, you can get it yourself!"
As Jesus is down walking on the water looking for the ball, a crowd has formed. One guy says, "Who does he think he is, Jesus Christ?"
"No," Moses says. "He thinks he's Tiger Woods."

Faithful Saints never lose their joyful smile.

Monday, December 6, 2021

Revelation 1:18
18 I am the Living One; I was dead, and now look, I am
alive for ever and ever! And I hold the keys of death and
Hades.

Reflection:
      This passage says a lot in just a few words. We can
get so caught up in our daily lives, that we become fearful
of all the evil and bad things that are happening around us.
What we need to remember is that God and Jesus are in
charge. If we are Christians, then we believe we have
found comfort. We know we will have life after death and
be with our Lord, and that we will live again. We are not
afraid of death, we look forward to the time we will be
with our Lord and Savior.

Prayer:
      Dear Heavenly Father, thank you for bringing us
the comfort we need in this cruel world. We are in the
midst of it all, and we see it all, but you have given us your
Son so he can live with you in Heaven. Thank you for all
you do for us. In your Son's name we pray, amen.

Tuesday, December 7, 2021

Carol Parker

Matthew 25:40
40 "The King will reply, 'Truly I tell you, whatever you did for one of the least of these brothers and sisters of mine, you did for me.'

Reflection:

Advent is a time for us to prepare for the coming of Christ as a baby. It is a time for me to be reminded that although Christ is always with me I need to make sure I'm putting into action what is expected of me. So often the business of living gets in the way of remembering what our Christian life should be centered upon. In our rush to prepare for the holidays we forget that reaching out to others in love is the real focus we should have.

In 1 Peter 3:8, we are reminded to "Live in harmony with one another, be sympathetic, love as brothers, be compassionate and humble". Then in Galatians 6:2 we are to "Carry each other's burdens." These are not messages just for the Advent season but for every day, all year, every year. Being compassionate, kind, gentle, patient, and humble are all attributes we should strive for and put into action.

So, as I strive to live the life that God wants me to live, I would challenge you to take some time during this Advent season's rush to see how you can share God's love and his way of life.

Prayer:

Dear Heavenly Father, we thank you for all the many blessings you have given us and also for the strength to face the challenges we have. Be with us now during the Advent season and also throughout the year as we strive to show your love to others. Help us to be your hands here on Earth. Amen.

Wednesday, December 8, 2021

Cindy Chambers
(Lay Servant)

Genesis 49:9-10
9 You are a lion's cub, Judah; you return from the prey, my son. Like a lion he crouches and lies down, like a lioness— who dares to rouse him? **10** The scepter will not depart from Judah, nor the ruler's staff from between his feet, until he to whom it belongs shall come and the obedience of the nations shall be his.

Reflection:
Our Bible verse is part of Jacob's blessings to his sons, based on their lives so far and what he perceives of the future. By using symbols of royalty, Jacob is saying to Judah that he is a king's son; his lineage will be that of royalty. WOW! Judah was seen as a leader due to actions he had taken in his life. His leadership was not that of violence like his two elder brothers, but a more positive one. While in this country we may not have royalty, we understand positive leadership. Now, if we turn to Matthew 1: 1-3a we see thirty-six generations later, the name of Jesus; the one to whom the scepter belongs; our ultimate leader and king.
When you read fairy tales, did you ever dream of being a prince or princess? I know I did. So, here might be some good news; we can continue to see ourselves as princes and princesses. Now before you start adding jeweled necklaces and diamond cuff links to your Christmas list, and start looking at real estate for that mansion, let's think about what that might mean. It's not

a rich living lifestyle we should be pursuing, but one of sharing. We are children of God, our King and Loving Father. We accept Jesus, the Prince of Peace, as our Savior calling ourselves brothers and sisters in His name. As such we are also putting ourselves in the role of leaders. Our lives should reflect that of Jesus. Let people see how wonderful life can be when we act justly, kindly, and selflessly. As we prepare to celebrate Christmas, let the lights we hang remind us, once again, that we are to reflect the true light of Jesus into the world. Let's make this Christmas another joy-filled holy day.

Prayer:

Lord, thank you for the worthy leaders before us. Help us continue that leadership and pass it on to the next generation. May our actions share your love for your children. In all our giving and receiving this Christmas, let our focus be not on items, but that we are celebrating you. Amen.

Thursday, December 9, 2021

Matt 11:28-30
Come unto me, all ye who are weary and burdened and I will give you rest. Take my yoke upon you and learn of me, for I am gentle and humble in heart, and you will find rest for your souls...For my yoke is easy and my burden is light.

Reflection:
This scripture was not just a reminder to Jesus' disciples but as an admonition for us today, to us who have accepted Him as our Savior. We must focus on following in His footsteps, for only through Jesus can we see the Father. Also, following Jesus means we accept the words of the Scriptures.

It is plain we will have burdens to bear, but we are not to carry them alone. Jesus said, "Take my yoke upon you and learn of me." The term *yoke* refers to a device to be used by a team of two. You may remember seeing a picture of a yoke on a team of oxen as the two shouldered the same load, both pulling at the same time. One cannot go ahead of the other, but the strength of the stronger one helps the weaker ox to share the load. The yoke was designed to bring the strength of the two animals together to pull a load that was impossible for one to pull on its own.

Prayer:
In our daily lives we have many challenges, perhaps some more than others. But we must remember the

words of Jesus. "Come unto Me....Take my yoke upon you...I will share your load and make your burden light." Humbly do His will and allow Him to guide and direct our lives. Amen.

Friday, December 10, 2021

Galen Miller

Colossians 3:17
17 And whatever you do, whether in word or deed, do it all in the name of the Lord Jesus, giving thanks to God the Father through him.

Reflection:
"Whatsoever ye do in **word or deed**."
      These words cover our daily lives, from day-to-day throughout our lives.
Am I at home? With family or friends? On the job where things can get stressful? On the road where I can come into situations that affect me adversely? In public places where I have no control of those surrounding me? Am I within a day where everything goes wrong?
The author of these words in Colossians 3:17 instructs me to rise above myself, give control to the HOLY SPIRIT dwelling within me.
      Take the opportunity to express and show that we do not have to yield to our inappropriate impulses. I do not need to respond in negative ways that do not show the will of GOD.

Prayer:
      Heavenly Father, thank you that we do not have to rely upon our own strength to live up to this admonition. Thank you that you have given to us the HOLY SPIRIT who will fill our being with knowledge and strength to do your will. Thank you that you have given to us an advocate to YOU in JESUS, THE CHRIST. We can come into your

presence to ask for, and receive forgiveness for not pleasing you. Forgiveness and strength can be ours by relying on JESUS. Amen.

Saturday, December 11, 2021

Kathy Ryan
(Lay Minister)

Ephesians 5:15-17
[15] Be very careful, then, how you live—not as unwise but as wise, [16] making the most of every opportunity, because the days are evil. [17] Therefore do not be foolish, but understand what the Lord's will is.

Reflection:
This passage always seems to put life in perspective for me. Paul is telling the Ephesians to be careful about the way they live. In the early church, a lot of Christians thought that they were made perfect because they had accepted Jesus Christ as their Lord and Savior. And wouldn't that be wonderful if that were really the way things were. We would be above everyone else, and could not do anything wrong. Paul is warning them there is a lot more to it. To be Christ-like, we have to be careful about the way we live each day. Christians are not above anyone, but through their example we need to make sure we are living a life that others want to emulate so we can be the model for their lives. As Christians we need to make the most of every opportunity to be better. And, we need to do this because the days are evil and Paul is warning that it is easy to be sucked in to the evil. We need to make sure we are leading a real Christian life. We need to be the disciples of our Lord and Savior to fulfill our mission as Christians, to make disciples of others.

Prayer:
Father God, we praise you and thank you for everything you do for each and every one of us. As the passage says, Lord, keep us from becoming too full of ourselves as we grow closer to you. Help us continue our Christian walk and help us to become the best we can be so we are the example you want us to be to grow your disciples. In Jesus' name we pray, amen.

Sunday, December 12, 2021

Psalm 118:24
The LORD has done it this very day; let us rejoice today and be glad.

Enjoy your Sunday worship!

Sunday Humor

Bent over and obviously in pain, the old man with a cane hobbled laboriously through the sanctuary and into the pastor's office while the choir was practicing.
Ten minutes later he came out, walking upright and moving with grace and speed.
"Good gracious," the choir director exclaimed. "Did the pastor heal you by faith?"
"No," the old man said with a smile.

"He just gave me a cane that wasn't six inches too short!"

Faithful Saints never lose their joyful smile.

Monday December 13, 2021

Kevin Costa

John 1:9-10
9 The true light that gives light to everyone was coming into the world. **10** He was in the world, and though the world was made through him, the world did not recognize him.

Reflection:

This passage, so early in the Gospel according to John, reminds me of the ways we don't readily see God's blessing — his light — when, in fact, it is always all around us. This past year was tough. My beloved mother died in August, and her passing was preceded by a lengthy decline. She was back and forth to the hospital for six months, and with each visit, her baseline health worsened. I prayed, of course, for her daily, and I wanted so badly for her to recover not just her health but her independence, vitality, and good spirits. These never came. Still, I prayed and prayed, but in late July, she made the decision to accept palliative care and enter hospice. Within a week, my mother was with God.

The death of any loved one is a dark, difficult time. But we will all die. While we might see a loved one's death, initially, as reason to think God *hasn't* heard our prayers, we are not recognizing Him in our midst. We are not seeing His light. How is this so?

My mother lived to be 89 years old. In her life, she endured many struggles. She was the daughter of immigrants who lived barely above the poverty line. She was forced to quit school in the tenth grade, despite her promise as a student, so that she could earn for her family. This was heartbreaking. But she married a wonderful man — my father — and they lived as man and wife for fifty years before my father's passing in 2002. She enjoyed independence, a loving extended family, and her grandson (my boy), Ethan.

This past February, however, landed her in the hospital with atrial fibrillation, and then a series of systems failures. I was anxious, frequently on a plane headed to Rhode Island, and helpless. When the call came in that she decided on palliative care, I prayed — as hard as I ever have — to know if this was the right decision. Didn't we have other options? Had we given up too soon? Isn't there a path to recovery?

And in the midst of my prayer came comfort — it's hard to say just how this happened. The clutch of deep anxiety simply eased. I realized that God not only had taken care of my mother; he had taken care of me, too. How lucky was I to be in a position to simply hop on a plane and be by her bedside when she needed me? How lucky was I to spend the final full week of my mother's life by her side in hospice? How lucky was I that my mother was . . . *my mother*? Of all the many other possible lives I could have lived, I was living *this* one — with love, with faith, with Kate and Ethan — and the son of the most wonderful mom I could ask for.

We will all die; that is certain. My prayers didn't extend my mother's life past the day God had named for her, but they were still answered. His light was surrounding me, but recognizing the light takes practice. Once I opened my eyes to see the blessings that gave me the way to be with my mother this past year, I couldn't help but be deeply grateful for all of God's love, protection, and grace.

Prayer:

Lord, we know that your light surrounds us every day. We know that our daily struggles and distractions cause us not to recognize your love right away. Lord, give us the eyes to see your light, however it shines, and give us the will to practice seeing your grace in the many ways you offer it to your people. We pray for your love and mercy. Amen.

Tuesday, December 14, 2021

Marlene Stivers

Isaiah 7:14
14 Therefore the Lord himself will give you a sign: The virgin will conceive and give birth to a son, and will call him Immanuel.

Reflection:
        To review my beliefs, I don't need special signs. I often know the reverse when times are tough or the weather is horrible. I often say, "What's the Lord trying to tell us?"
It's up to us to research our thoughts to profit from God's signs in our praising of his gifts, wisdom and knowledge. I reflect on all my blessings as signs of his love. This keeps me on the straight and narrow and shows other people that I am one of God's people. We just need to look and listen as told in Isaiah 7:14.

Prayer:
Lord, as I live each day in your way, I pray to be able to recognize your blessing and directions for me to understand all the signs that you have given me. For I am happy and proud to be one of your people. Amen.

Wednesday, December 15, 2021

Melinda Dettmer
(Nurture Committee Chair)

Genesis 22:18
18 and through your offspring all nations on earth will be blessed, because you have obeyed me."

Reflection:
This is just one example of God honoring those who honor him.

After reading this verse, I reflected on how the people of biblical times used to honor God. They would make long trips to their place of worship, treating it with great respect as they were on holy ground, offering up burnt offerings, tithing, some even gave up their offspring to serve the Lord. The people of biblical times feared God and had a lot of respect for him and made huge sacrifices to honor God.

When my parents were growing up, life was centered around the church. There were lots of activities at church. Everything was closed on Sundays, you did not work. Sabbath was observed. Sundays were a day of worship and rest. You would put on your Sunday best to attend church as you were honoring God. Tithing was a financial sacrifice.

Nowadays, society is busy juggling schedules trying to balance school activities, work schedules, sporting events and church activities. With church and church activities often taking

second priority. Sunday best clothing has been replaced with a more relaxed and comfortable
wardrobe. Some churches have coffee bars to entice worshipers to get up and get to church.
Tithing for many has become less of a sacrifice and more what we can comfortably contribute
or what we happen to have in the wallet that day.

God hasn't changed. What has changed?

Advent and Christmas are a time of worship and celebration of the birth of Christ. Often
over shadowed by the pageantry, decoration, festivities and gifts associated with the Christmas
season. As we celebrate advent and prepare to celebrate the birth of Christ, let us take time to
reflect on how we honor God. Let us stay focused on the reason for the season and
honor God and the birth of Christ.

Prayer:

Dear Lord, you are a loving and merciful Lord, and we are grateful! So often we get wrapped up in our busy schedules and deadlines that we fail to keep you first in our priorities. This holiday season help us to remember it's not the number of gifts, the glitter of the decorations, or the time spent at holiday parties that are important.
It is your gift to us and our time spent with you! Amen.

Thursday, December 16, 2021

Myron Horn
(Lay Servant)

1 Kings 19:11-13
"Go out and stand before me on the mountain," the Lord
told him. And as Elijah stood there, the Lord passed by,
and a mighty windstorm hit the mountain. It was such a
terrible blast that the rocks were torn loose, but the Lord
was not in the wind. After the wind there was an
earthquake, but the Lord was not in the earthquake. And
after the earthquake there was a fire, but the Lord was not
in the fire. And after the fire there was the sound of a
gentle whisper. When Elijah heard it, he wrapped his face
in his cloak and went out and stood at the entrance to the
cave.

Reflection:
As a police officer, I was trained to use a still, quiet
voice to respond to a domestic disturbance. Such a voice
would often cause those trying to communicate by yelling
to stop and listen. Sure, the Lord could talk to us in a great
rumble of thunder or the force of a great wind, but would
we listen? Instead, God chooses to talk to you in a quiet
way. It forces us to settle down, and actively listen for that
quiet whisper, that still, quiet voice, that gentle nudge of
the Holy Spirit. The question should not be "Is God talking
to you?" It should be, "Are you listening to Him?"

Prayer:
O Heavenly Father, help us to learn to listen for
your guidance. Slow our lives down, so that we can find a

quiet moment for prayer and reflection. Grant that we recognize you not in the thunder and the earthquake, but in that soft voice that will speak to us in our time of need. Amen.

Friday, December 17, 2021

Patrick Chambers

Jeremiah 23:5-6
5 "The days are coming," declares the LORD, "when I will
raise up for David a righteous Branch, a King who will reign
wisely and do what is just and right in the land. **6** In his
days Judah will be saved and Israel will live in safety. This is
the name by which he will be called: The LORD Our
Righteous Savior.

Reflection:
       The first time I read this I was struck by one word
that doesn't really find a home with me, King. In the place
where I have grown up we do not have a King. I have
never lived under a king and in all honesty, with a fairly
broad knowledge of world history, I hope to never live
under a king. What then am I reading here? How do I see
the place where I am being led in this passage?
       When I was twenty-seven, I accepted the Christ. It
has been forty years since that terrifying day. Terrifying in
that I didn't know what would happen, I didn't know
where to go. But those forty years have been my life and I
have learned that I should not always focus on that part
with which I might have a problem but to instead see what
is there to help me through, to help me to grow.
       Jesus is the One who will and does reign wisely and
does what is just and right in the land. Judah and Israel
are real places full of real people and I am, we are, part of
those people. The scope of GOD'S work has grown beyond
the boundaries of Judah and Israel to where it now

encompasses the entire world and in the not too distant future will move to envelope other worlds. Awesome.

The task before us is immense but simple, love GOD and love others as we love ourselves and when asked the source of that love, use the name by which he will be called: The LORD Our Righteous Savior.

Prayer:

Thank you, GOD. Teach us, we pray, to always open our prayer with thankfulness on our lips and in our hearts. You sent your Son, Jesus, to be our LORD, to be Our Righteous Savior. Open our minds and our hearts that we can serve you and that we can accept your blessings so that we may, in turn, be a blessing. We pray in Jesus name, amen.

Saturday, December 18, 2021

Pauline Reisberg
(Steven Minister)

Isaiah 9:6
6 For to us a child is born, to us a son is given, and the
government will be on his shoulders. And he will be called
Wonderful Counselor, Mighty God, Everlasting Father,
Prince of Peace.

Reflection:
 As a young child, I couldn't wait for Christmas to
come. I looked forward to baking cookies, getting gifts,
and visiting with all my cousins. At home we had a small
Nativity that we displayed each year, and I loved placing
the figures in their places around the barn. In Sunday
school, I learned that Christmas was a time to celebrate
Jesus' birth. Along the way, I gradually learned the real
meaning of Christmas, that Jesus is a gift from God and he
was sent to earth to show us how to love God and love
one another. Most importantly, he would die for our sins
on the cross so that we might live in eternity with him.
 One experience stands out vividly in my memory.
As a teenager and member of Youth Fellowship, I looked
forward each year to participating in the Nativity on
Christmas Eve. One year I was asked to be Mary in the
pageant. That night as the lights dimmed in the sanctuary
and I held baby Jesus (a baby doll, of course), in my arms, a
feeling came over me. I thought about Mary on that first
Christmas Eve and how she must have felt knowing that
she just gave birth to the son of God. Is was a special time
for me.

Prayer:

Dear Heavenly Father, we thank you for fulfilling that long ago promise of sending the Messiah. Help us to prepare our hearts during this Advent season to once again receive that gift. May we pass on to others the love that Jesus showed us by loving God and loving one another.

Sunday, December 19, 2021

Psalm 118:24
The LORD has done it this very day; let us rejoice today and be glad.

Enjoy your Sunday worship!

Sunday Humor

After worship one Sunday a little boy told the pastor, "When I grow up, I'm going to give you some money." "Well, thank you," the pastor replied, "but why?"

"Because my daddy says you're one of the poorest preachers we've ever had."

Faithful Saints never lose their joyful smile.

Monday, December 20, 2021

Rachel Miller
(Music Director)

Micah 5:2
2 "But you, Bethlehem Ephrathah, though you are small among the clans of Judah, out of you will come for me one who will be ruler over Israel, whose origins are from of old, from ancient times."

Reflection:
"O little town of Bethlehem..."

This verse brings to mind a certain well-loved carol. "Bethlehem" is a word we hear often throughout advent. In our minds it is a very important place, the place where the savior was born. In the time of the eighth-century BCE prophet Micah however, Bethlehem was a very small, insignificant town. It was so insignificant that it was not named as one of the cities of Judah in Joshua 15. How is it that God has brought about such greatness in such an unimportant place?

There have been times in all of our lives when we have thought of ourselves as too small, too unskilled, too slow, too unimportant, or too unworthy to even be noticed by God. But God notices you even so. More than that, God *knows* you (completely, from the inside out) and God *loves* you. You are important to God even as insignificant as you may feel compared to the vast number of souls that have walked this earth.

God places value in the small and meek and lowly. Matthew 6:26 says, "[26]Look at the birds of the air; they neither sow nor reap nor gather into barns, and yet your heavenly Father feeds them. Are you not of more value than they?" God does not reserve his attention for the greatest and most powerful among us. In fact, our struggle to be great in our own right leads us away from God. Psalm 33:13,16 says "[13]The Lord looks down from heaven; he sees all humankind... [16]A king is not saved by his great army; a warrior is not delivered by his great strength." It is not on us to be great on our own, God can use us to do great things.

And even if God does not use us to change the world in quite such an earth-shattering way as he used the little town of Bethlehem, *greatness* can have many forms. Teaching a child; being there for a friend going through a tough time; acting as an example of Christ's love to a stranger; giving your time, money, talents, or prayers to those in need - these can all be acts of greatness. Though doing these things may not make us feel like superheroes, they are still examples of God working through us.

God sent his son to be human, like the rest of us. He chose a small town, Bethlehem, in which to come to Earth and a small woman, Mary, to give birth to the Messiah. And throughout his life, Jesus surrounded himself with small people. We are all small people, but no one is too small for God.

Prayer:
(Taken from verse 4 of O Little Town of Bethlehem by Phillip Brooks)
O holy Child of Bethlehem, descend to us, we pray;
cast out our sin, and enter in, be born in us today.
We hear the Christmas angels the great glad tidings tell;
O come to us, abide with us, our Lord Emmanuel!

Tuesday, December 21, 2021

Ron Weller
(Sunday School Teacher)

Isaiah 25:9
9 In that day they will say, "Surely this is our God; we trusted in him, and he saved us. This is the LORD, we trusted in him; let us rejoice and be glad in his salvation."

Reflection:

For as long as I can remember, I've been a people pleaser. From my early days around the house or at school, I always wanted to do the right thing. I wouldn't say it was anything exemplary about me, I just think it was in my nature. I liked making people happy.

Now that wasn't always a good thing, especially when I got to my teenage years, when being rebellious was sometimes the attractive option and staying out of trouble the opposite. I took my fair share of abuse for being the "good boy".

When I got out of college and started my career, I took the same approach to my work. I liked turning in good work but the fear of letting the boss down and making mistakes would get to me. I'd worry and the anxiety would lead to some sleepless nights. Sometimes it would get bad enough that the only refuge was turning to God. I'd recall the stories from the Bible when he provided over and over for those who were lost in ways both small and large. Now, when I feel the pangs of self-worry, I can pray for others who don't know of that salvation.

Prayer:

Father of peace, the story of the Bible is the story of salvation. What a joy to know of our blessed salvation that frees us from worry and leads to joyful thanksgiving. Amen.

Wednesday, December 22, 2021

1 Peter 5:7
Cast all your anxiety on him because he cares for you.

Reflection:

Anxiety is such a difficult emotion. Those feelings of stress, uneasiness, distress, and dread can be overwhelming. Recently I've watched my daughter struggle with anxiety. If we're not heading to the bus stop at the exact minute we tend to head out the door, she gets very upset and it's hard to calm her down. If she can't complete her math equations, she spins out of control and refuses to take a break and works herself into a deeply anxious state.

It physically pains me to see her so upset. I have always wanted my children to know that they don't have to work for my love, that they don't have to be any certain *way* to earn my love. I want them to be able to rest in my love and tell me what's wrong and know that no matter what, I will always love them and will always support them. That no matter what, we are in it together and I will always be there to help them find their way out of a problem. That nothing they've done is so bad that they can't tell me. That I will forgive them. I want them to be able to lay their troubles at my feet for a while and rest.

These feelings toward my children are so powerful and so strong, and they make me think that God's feelings toward us are even more powerful still. God loves us perfectly. We can lay our burdens and worries at his feet. His love is a place of peace and refuge, a place to rest. So, when we get caught up in anxiety and worry, God wants us to remember that he cares for us. He loves us. And he is strong enough to take all our burdens away.

Prayer:

   Lord, we are so prone to anxiety. Remind us, Lord, that we can place our worries at your feet, and you are strong enough to carry them for us. Remind us that you love us perfectly and we can rest in your love. We pray in your name, amen.

Thursday, December 23, 2021

Wayne Reisberg
(Steven Minister)

Luke 1:30-31
30 But the angel said to her, "Do not be afraid, Mary; you have found favor with God. **31** You will conceive and give birth to a son, and you are to call him Jesus.

Reflection:

Verse 30 lets Mary know that God knows her and cares for her. At age three, I was the new child from that other Methodist church where my mom grew up. But "Jesus Loves Me" and "The B-I-B-L-E" at Ward's Sunday School reassured me I was loved. Later, the felt board lesson on the Twenty-third Psalm assured me as the angel assured Mary, "Be not afraid." The Shepard dogs: Shirley (surely), Goodness, and Mercy would follow and protect me all the days of my life.

In verse 31, behold refers to a wonderful and extraordinary event in Mary's life that would bring a spiritual savior and eternal salvation. For an introverted teen with full confidence in God the Creator, but little in his own spiritual strength to go up for an altar call was frightening. As the organist played verse after verse of Just As I Am, I cam to the defining moment to go to the altar to dedicate myself to the Savior. I give thanks to the preacher's wife who started a youth choir and my vocal ministry to Christ. I give thanks for Sub zone counselors who initiated bonfires on spiritual retreats at Camp Manidokan which strengthened that dedication. I give thanks for Camp Hope Friday night sharing and other public and private re-dedication which has made the Savior real and eternal.

Prayer:

Lord, thank you for your love shone through the saints at Ward's Chapel that encouraged and loved an introverted child to be a Child of God. A-amen, a-amen, a-amen, a-amen, a-amen.

Friday, December 24, 2021

Wendy Miller
(Mission Committee Chair)

Luke 1:29-33 The Message (MSG)

She was thoroughly shaken, wondering what was behind a greeting like that. But the angel assured her, "Mary, you have nothing to fear. God has a surprise for you: You will become pregnant and give birth to a son and call his name Jesus. He will be great, be called 'Son of the Highest.' The Lord God will give him the throne of his father David; He will rule Jacob's house forever— no end, ever, to his kingdom."

Reflection:

On Christmas day of 1999, we told our two girls, almost 6 and 4, that they would have a new baby in the family. Our four-year-old, Hannah, told us that "mommy is having a boy and his name is Jacob." We would laugh and say, "wait and see" but in reality, my husband and I would discuss how we would never name our son Jacob and give him the last name Miller--way too many Jacob Millers in the world already!

Fast forward a few months later and we find out we are indeed having a boy! We are all excited but no one more than Hannah. She continues to insist his name will be Jacob and each time I tease her and say no, so she is not disappointed when we name him something different. Months come and go and we still can't decide on a good name. My husband and I agreed we might have to meet the little guy first. Hannah is still Team Jacob!

Finally, August 2000 arrives and we get to meet our big, little boy and we have not chosen a firm name---but still siding with Team NOT Jacob! My husband leaves the room to call the grandparents to announce that he has arrived healthy and adorable, but still no name. The baby and I are there together recovering from our journey. The big bundle of boy begins to wiggle and fuss and before I know it, these words come out of my mouth, "Shh, shh, shh, it's OK, Jacob, mommy is right here!" My husband returns to me laughing, and when he hears my story, we both decide that maybe, just maybe it was meant to be!

This is the first story I thought about when I read Luke 1:32-33 from the Message. I never believed that I would have a son named Jacob based on a prediction of a four-year-old. And I think of Mary, a young woman, being told by an angel that she will give birth to a boy, is given his name, and is told that he will sit on David's throne and rule over the descendants of Jacob forever and ever! If you are familiar with this story then you know that Mary accepted this as truth, saying she was a servant of the Lord. How wonderful it must have been for Mary to receive this news and believe it so easily! What simple faith she must have had to believe knowing that she may be gossiped about. This Christmas, I hope you can believe that "Nothing is Impossible for God!" Mary believed and was ready to face the consequences. She said yes---yes to God, yes to the impossible.

Prayer:

Dear Heavenly Father, we pray this advent season that we listen to what you have to say to us. That our faith leads us to say YES to you and YES to your plan. Help us to believe that nothing is impossible for you! May we look forward to the Christmas celebration and experience the joy that Jesus' birth brought to Mary and brings to us today. In Jesus' name, amen.

Made in the USA
Middletown, DE
23 November 2021

53304719R00031